MY FIRST SPORTS

Wrestling

by Ellen Frazel

BLASTOFF! READERS 4

BELLWETHER MEDIA • MINNEAPOLIS, MN

Note to Librarians, Teachers, and Parents:

Blastoff! Readers are carefully developed by literacy experts and combine standards-based content with developmentally appropriate text.

Level 1 provides the most support through repetition of high-frequency words, light text, predictable sentence patterns, and strong visual support.

Level 2 offers early readers a bit more challenge through varied simple sentences, increased text load, and less repetition of high-frequency words.

Level 3 advances early-fluent readers toward fluency through increased text and concept load, less reliance on visuals, longer sentences, and more literary language.

Level 4 builds reading stamina by providing more text per page, increased use of punctuation, greater variation in sentence patterns, and increasingly challenging vocabulary.

Level 5 encourages children to move from "learning to read" to "reading to learn" by providing even more text, varied writing styles, and less familiar topics.

Whichever book is right for your reader, Blastoff! Readers are the perfect books to build confidence and encourage a love of reading that will last a lifetime!

This edition first published in 2011 by Bellwether Media, Inc.

No part of this publication may be reproduced in whole or in part without written permission of the publisher. For information regarding permission, write to Bellwether Media, Inc., Attention: Permissions Department, 5357 Penn Avenue South, Minneapolis, MN 55419.

Library of Congress Cataloging-in-Publication Data
Frazel, Ellen.
Wrestling / by Ellen Frazel.
   p. cm. – (Blastoff! readers : my first sports)
Includes bibliographical references and index.
Summary: "Simple text and full-color photographs introduce beginning readers to the sport of wrestling. Developed by literacy experts for students in grades two through five"–Provided by publisher.
ISBN 978-1-60014-571-1 (hardcover : alk. paper)
1. Wrestling–Juvenile literature. I. Title.
GV1195.3.F73 2011
796.812092–dc22
   [B]   2010035457

Printed in the United States of America, North Mankato, MN.
010111   1176

Contents

What Is Wrestling?   4

The Basic Rules of Wrestling   8

Wrestling Gear   16

Wrestling Today   20

Glossary   22

To Learn More   23

Index   24

What Is Wrestling?

Wrestling is a **martial art** in which two people **grapple** to try to overpower each other. This martial art has been around for thousands of years. People in ancient Egypt, Greece, and Rome practiced different forms of wrestling.

fun fact

Greco-Roman and freestyle wrestling are the two styles practiced by men in the Summer Olympics.

In the 1880s, wrestling became an organized sport in the United States. The first college wrestling meet was held in 1903. Today, middle and high school students practice **scholastic wrestling**. This form is known as **folkstyle**. It is a combination of many wrestling styles brought to the U.S. from Europe.

The Basic Rules of Wrestling

nelson hold

The goal of wrestling is to **pin** an opponent on a mat. Wrestlers use **nelson holds** and other moves to do this.

A wrestler's shoulders or shoulder blades must touch the mat for two seconds for a pin to count. A referee slaps the mat when a wrestler has been pinned.

fun fact

Wrestlers move quickly during a match. The referee must be ready to drop to the mat and watch for a pin at any moment.

neutral position

! **fun fact**
Wrestlers are organized into weight classes. They only face opponents who weigh about the same as them.

A scholastic wrestling match has three two-minute periods. Two wrestlers start a match standing across from each other. This is called the **neutral position**.

In the second period, one wrestler chooses the starting position. He or she can pick the neutral position or the **referee's position**. In the third period, the other wrestler picks a starting position.

referee's position

Wrestlers can win a match by **fall** with a pin. They can also win by scoring points. They win by **technical fall** if they lead by 15 points in any period.

At the end of the third period, wrestlers can win by **decision** if they are still ahead in points. They win by **major decision** if they lead by 8 or more points.

! fun fact

Some matches go into overtime. In a one-minute sudden victory period, the first wrestler to score a point is the winner!

Scoring Points

Move	Starting Position	Description	Point Value
Takedown	Neutral	wrestler brings opponent down to the mat	2
Escape	Defensive	wrestler escapes and gets back to the neutral position	1
Reversal	Defensive	wrestler escapes and puts opponent in the defensive position	2
Near Fall	Offensive	wrestler holds opponent's shoulder on the mat, or both shoulders 4 inches (10 centimeters) from the mat	2-4, depending on how many seconds the move lasts

Wrestlers earn points based on positions and moves. In the referee's position, defensive wrestlers must escape their opponent. Offensive wrestlers try to bring their opponent farther down to the mat.

offensive wrestler

defensive wrestler

Wrestling Gear

headgear →

singlet →

Wrestlers wear headgear and special uniforms. Headgear protects a wrestler's ears during a match.

A one-piece wrestling uniform is called a **singlet**. It fits tightly against a wrestler's body so an opponent cannot grab at it. Shoes with rubber soles help a wrestler grip the mat.

A wrestling mat is made of thick, stiff material. The wrestling area is a circle that is at least 28 feet (8.5 meters) wide.

Most of the match takes place in an inner circle. This circle is 10 feet (3 meters) wide. It has two starting lines that are 12 inches (30.5 centimeters) apart.

inner circle

10 feet

28 feet

wrestling mat

Wrestling Today

Clarissa Chun

Millions of people around the world wrestle today. Since 1921, the International Federation of Associated Wrestling Styles has managed the sport.

Wrestlers like Clarissa Chun, Randi Miller, and Henry Cejudo competed for the U.S. in the 2008 **Summer Olympics**. Cejudo became the youngest American wrestler to win Olympic gold. He was only 21 years old! Could you be the next young champion?

Henry Cejudo

!

fun fact

Freestyle is the only wrestling style practiced by women at the international level. It was first included in the Summer Olympics in 2004.

Glossary

decision—a way to win a match; a wrestler ahead by fewer than 8 points at the end of the third period wins by decision.

fall—when a wrestler pins his or her opponent; a fall ends a match in any period.

folkstyle—the wrestling style practiced at school levels in the United States; folkstyle grew out of different wrestling styles practiced in the early history of the U.S.

grapple—to use the body to try to gain a physical advantage over someone

major decision—a way to win a match; a wrestler ahead by 8 or more points at the end of the third period wins by major decision.

martial art—a style of fighting and self-defense

nelson holds—moves where wrestlers try to put their arms under their opponent's armpits and push on their opponent's neck; nelson holds help wrestlers pin their opponent.

neutral position—a starting position where two wrestlers stand behind their starting lines and face each other

pin—when a wrestler holds an opponent's shoulders or shoulder blades to the mat for two seconds

referee's position—a starting position where there is a defensive and offensive wrestler; the defensive wrestler starts on his or her hands and knees below the offensive wrestler.

scholastic wrestling—the name for wrestling practiced in middle and high schools across the United States

singlet—the one-piece uniform a wrestler wears during a match

Summer Olympics—a worldwide sporting event held every four years in the summer

technical fall—when a wrestler leads by 15 points; a technical fall ends a match in any period.

To Learn More

AT THE LIBRARY

Crossingham, John. *Wrestling in Action*. New York, N.Y.: Crabtree Pub. Co., 2003.

Ditchfield, Christin. *Wrestling*. New York, N.Y.: Children's Press, 2000.

Ryan, Thomas, and Julia Sampson. *Beginning Wrestling*. New York, N.Y.: Sterling Pub., 2001.

ON THE WEB
Learning more about wrestling is as easy as 1, 2, 3.

1. Go to www.factsurfer.com.

2. Enter "wrestling" into the search box.

3. Click the "Surf" button and you will see a list of related Web sites.

With factsurfer.com, finding more information is just a click away.

Index

1880s, 6
1903, 6
1921, 20
2004, 21
2008, 21
Cejudo, Henry, 21
Chun, Clarissa, 20, 21
decision, 13
defensive wrestler, 14, 15
Europe, 6
fall, 12
folkstyle, 6
freestyle wrestling, 5, 21
grapple, 5
Greco-Roman wrestling, 5
headgear, 16, 17
inner circle, 19
International Federation
    of Associated Wrestling
    Styles, 20
major decision, 13
martial art, 5
mat, 8, 9, 14, 17, 18, 19
Miller, Randi, 21
nelson holds, 8

neutral position, 10, 11
offensive wrestler, 14, 15
overtime, 13
periods, 10, 11, 13
pin, 8, 9, 12
points, 12, 13, 14
referee, 9
referee's position, 11, 14
scholastic wrestling, 6, 10
singlet, 16, 17
Summer Olympics, 5, 21
technical fall, 12
United States, 6, 21
weight classes, 10

The images in this book are reproduced through the courtesy of: Charles T. Bennett, front cover; Nicholas Piccillo, front cover (small); Al Bello/Getty Images, pp. 4-5; Corbey R. Dorsey/NCAA Photos/AP Images, pp. 6-7; Carolyn Kaster/AP Images, p. 8; Bob Zellar/AP Images, p. 9; Mehmet Can, p. 10; Dennis MacDonald/Alamy, pp. 11, 15; Randy Snyder/AP Images, pp. 12, 16-17; Steve Pope/AP Images, p. 13; Sports Illustrated/Getty Images, pp. 18, 21; J. Lethal, p. 19; AFP/Getty Images, p. 20.